COMPASSIONATE APPOINTMENT- SERVICE MATTERS SUPREME COURT'S LATEST LEADING CASE LAWS

CASE NOTES- FACTS- FINDINGS OF APEX COURT JUDGES & CITATIONS

JAYPRAKASH BANSILAL SOMANI

ISBN 979-888569189-5

Dedicated

To

All the Past & Present Judges of the Supreme Court of India.

Salute to their wisdom.

Salute to their interpretation of Law.

Salute to their elaborative judgement writing.

Contents

Preface

Dear Learned Advocates of the Trial Courts, Tribunals, Appellate Tribunals, High Courts, Supreme Court, HR Professionals, Corporates, Govt Recruitment Officers & Employees,

I am very delighted to provide you a book on 'Compassionate Appointment- Service Matters' - Supreme Court of India's Latest Leading Case Laws'.

In this book you will get...

1. Name of the Case i. e. Cause title

2.Relevant Sections discussed in the case

3.Hon'ble Judges/Coram of the case

4.Number of PDF Pages in Original Judgement of the case

5. All available Citations of the case

6. Case Note with appeal allowed/ dismissed or disposed off

7. Facts of the case

8.Hon'ble Apex Court's findings, while dismissing/allowing or disposing the appeal

9. Ratio Decidendi if any.

My special thanks to Manupatra, because of their web portal I can compile this book in well manner. I am also thankful to Notion Press to support me to publish & market this book throughout the Country. Thanks to my Juniors, Advocate Colleagues & Insolvency Professional Colleagues to support me in this venture.

Miss Devpriya Shah has helped me a lot to compile this book.

I hope this book will add some value addition in the wealth of your legal knowledge. Your positive feedbacks will boost me to compile/ write further books & negative feedbacks will improve my skills. Kindly send your valuable feedbacks by email.

Thanks with Regards,

Jayprakash B. Somani

Advocate, Supreme Court of India

Email: jaysomani64@gmail.com

Web Site:www.jayprakashsomani.com

Call: 8384051134, 9322188701, 9318381287

Acknowledgements

Printed & Published by

Notion Press

No. 8, 3rd Cross Street,
CIT Colony, Mylapore,
Chennai, Tamil Nadu- 600004

ᑭᑭᑭ

Managed by

Jayprakash Somani Advocates & Solicitors

Law Firm for Supreme Court of India

Delhi Office

257 C, Pocket 1, Mayur Vihar Phase 1, Delhi 110091.
Call 8384051134, 9322188701, 8459194576, 01141051516

Supreme Court Chamber

312, 3rd Floor, M. C. Setalvad Block, In front of 'D' Gate, Bhagwan Das Road, Supreme Court of India, New Delhi 110001
Contact: 8459194576, 9811011747

www.jayprakashsomani.com

ᑭᑭᑭ

Books are available online at

1. **Notion Press:** https://notionpress.com/author/jayprakash_somani
2. **Amazon:** https://www.amazon.in/s?k=jayprakash+somani
3. **Flipkart:** https://www.flipkart.com/search?q=Jayprakash%20Somani

ᑭᑭᑭ

ONE

The Director of Treasuries in Karnataka and Ors. Vs. V. Somyashree, 2021

Hon'ble Judges/Coram:

M.R. Shah and Aniruddha Bose, JJ.

Equivalent Citation:

2021(8)ADJ665, (2021)IVLLJ286SC, 2021(II)OLR838, 2021(4)SCT98(SC), MANU/SC/0631/2021

Relevant Section/provisions: Article 14 and Article 16 of Constitution of India

Number of Pages in the Original Judgment: 4

Case Note:

Service - Compassionate Appointment - Rights of divorced daughter - Determination thereof - Rule 3(2)(ii) of Karnataka Civil Services (Appointment on Compassionate Grounds) Rules 1996 (Rules) - Whether divorced daughter has right to seek compassionate appointment?

Facts:

Mother of the original writ Petitioner was employed with the Government of Karnataka as Second Division Assistant. She died. Original writ Petitioner at the relevant time was a married daughter initiated a divorce proceedings for divorce. Decree was passed. On the very next day she submitted an application to appoint her on compassionate ground on the death of her mother. Application was rejected on the ground that there is no provision of compassionate appointment for divorced daughter. Challenge made before Tribunal after about two years of rejection. Application was dismissed. By impugned judgment High Court allowed the Writ and quashed and set aside the order passed by the Tribunal.

Held, while allowing the Appeal:

At the relevant time when the deceased employee died and when the original writ Petitioner-Respondent herein made an application for appointment on compassionate ground the 'divorced daughter' were not eligible for appointment on compassionate ground and the 'divorced daughter' was not within the definition of 'dependent.' The Respondent herein-original writ Petitioner at that time was a married daughter. Her marriage was subsisting on the date of the death of the deceased. The chronology of dates and events would suggest that only for the purpose of getting appointment on compassionate ground the decree of divorce by mutual consent has been obtained.

Appeal allowed. The impugned common judgment and order quashed and set aside.

PPP

TWO

THE STATE OF UTTAR PRADESH AND ORS. VS. PREMLATA, 2021

Hon'ble Judges/Coram:

M.R. Shah and A.S. Bopanna, JJ.

Equivalent Citation:

2021(10)ADJ403, 2021(4)SCT266(SC), MANU/SC/0787/2021

Relevant Sections: Article 14 and Article 16 of Constitution of India; Rule 5 and rule 8 of Dying-In-Harness Rules 1974; Uttar Pradesh Radio AdhinasthSewa Second Amendment Niyamawali, 2005

Number of Pages in the Original Judgment: 5

Case Note:

Service - Compassionate Appointment - Decease Class IV employee - Wife though offered job but refused - In other job, she could not clear physical fitness - Next, what she offered was in Class-III - Her application was accordingly rejected - Writ initiated by her allowed - In appeal, High Court vide impugned judgment set aside the claim of Respondent - Hence, the present appeal – Whether the impugned judgment rightly directed Appellants to consider Respondent's candidature?

Facts:

The deceased employee at the time of his death was serving as Messenger in Police Radio Department of Uttar Pradesh (Class-IV). The Respondent being widow of the deceased sought appointment on compassionate ground which was rejected on the ground of not fulfilling the requisite eligibility criteria for the post opted. In another application submitted, she could not clear the physical fitness examination. Respondent was instead offered the post relevant. Instead of accepting the said post, Respondent filed writ claiming the appointment on the post of Workshop Hand (KarmshalaKarmchari) in Police Radio Department under the provisions of Dying- In-Harness Rules 1974 (Rules 1974). Petition was dismissed on the ground that as the deceased employee was Class-IV employee and she has also been offered appointment on a Class-IV post. She cannot claim appointment on compassionate ground on the post of Workshop Hand or on any other suitable Class-III post.

Held, while allowing the Appeal:

Compassionate appointment is an exception to the general Rule of appointment in the public services and is in favour of the dependents of a deceased dying in harness. The whole object of granting compassionate employment is to enable the family to tide over the sudden crisis. The object is not to give such family a post much less a post held by the deceased. Appellants were justified in offering the appointment to the Respondent on the post of Messenger. However, the Respondent refused the appointment on such post. Division Bench of the High Court has misinterpreted and misconstrued Rule 5 of the Rules 1974 and in observing and holding that the 'suitable post' under Rule 5 of the Dying-In-Harness Rules 1974 would mean any post suitable to the qualification of the candidate and the appointment on compassionate ground is to be offered considering the educational qualification of the dependent. Such an interpretation would defeat the object and purpose of appointment on compassionate ground. In view of the above present appeal succeeds. The impugned judgment and order passed by the Division Bench of the High Court quashed and set aside.

THREE

The State of Kerala and Ors. Vs. Leesamma Joseph, 2021

Hon'ble Judges/Coram:

Sanjay Kishan Kaul and R. Subhash Reddy, JJ.

Equivalent Citation:

AIR2021SC3076, 2021(5)ALD42, 2021(4)ALT122, 2021 3 AWC2858SC, 2021(4)BLJ280, 2021(II)CLR695, 2021(2)ESC594(SC), [2021(170)FLR696], 2021(3)J.L.J.R.66, 2021(3)JLJ137, 2021 (4) KHC 318, 2021(4)KLT191, 2021LabIC3105, 2021(6)MhLj1, (2021)5MLJ196, 2021(4)MPLJ325, 2021(3)PLJR58, 2021(3)SCT189(SC), 2021(5)SLR811(SC), MANU/SC/0385/2021

Relevant sections/provisions: Section 33 and 327 of the Persons with Disabilities (Equal Opportunities, Protection of Rights and Full Participation) Act, 1995 (1995 Act), The Rights of Persons with Disabilities Act, 2016.

Number of Pages in the Original Judgment: 10

Case Note:

Service - Promotion - Rights and equal opportunities - Persons with special abilities (PWD) - The Persons with Disabilities (Equal Opportunities, Protection of Rights and Full Participation) Act, 1995 (1995 Act) - The Rights of Persons with Disabilities Act, 2016 (2016 Act) that replaced the 1995 Act - Impugned order decided in favour of Respondent on her right of promotion under the 1995 Act - Whether the 1995 Act mandates reservations in promotions for persons with disabilities? - Whether reservation under Section 33 of the 1995 Act is dependent upon identification of posts as stipulated by Section 32?

Facts:

Respondent was appointed on compassionate grounds, after her brother had passed away during service. She undisputedly suffered from Post Polio Residual Paralysis (L) Lower Limb and her permanent disability was assessed at 55%. The Respondent subsequently cleared all departmental tests for promotion, and was given due promotions. The issue raised by the Respondent was pertaining to her entitlement to promotions with all consequential benefits under the 1995 Act as she suffered from physical disability. Tribunal dismissed the application seeking relief sought. High Court set aside order of the Tribunal. Hence, the present appeal.

Held, while dismissing the Appeals:

i. What is required is identification of posts in every establishment until exempted under proviso to Section 33. No doubt the identification of the posts was a prerequisite to appointment, but then the appointment cannot be frustrated by refusing to comply with the prerequisite.

i. The 1995 Act does not make a distinction between a person who may have entered service on account of disability and a person who may have acquired disability after having entered the service. Similarly, the same position would be with the person who may have entered service on a claim of a compassionate appointment. The mode of entry in service cannot be a ground to make out a case of discriminatory promotion.

iii. The course of action followed by the High Court in the impugned order is salutary and does not call for any interference. In fact, what seems to emerge is that the Appellant-State has not implemented the judgment of this Court in Rajeev Kumar Gupta's and Siddaraju's cases. Thus, directions issued to the State of Kerala to implement these judgments and provide for reservation in promotion in all posts after identifying said posts. This exercise should be completed within a period of three months.

iv. The appeal is accordingly dismissed in terms aforesaid.

FOUR

MUNISH KUMAR VS. STATE OF HIMACHAL PRADESH AND ORS., 2020

Hon'ble Judges/Coram:

Dr. D.Y. Chandrachud, Hemant Gupta and Ajay Rastogi, JJ.

Equivalent Citation:

2020(3)SCT496(SC), MANU/SC/0536/2020

Relevant sections/provisions: Rule 38 of the CCS (Pension) Rules 1972

Number of Pages in the Original Judgment: 2

Case Note:

Service - Compassionate Appointment - Rule 38 of the CCS (Pension) Rules 1972 - Appellant's father applied for retirement on medical grounds - Application allowed after the death of Appellant's father - Appellant's application for compassionate appointment rejected as being not applicable - Whether Appellant's application for compassionate appointment rightly rejected on the ground that in the case of a government servant retiring on medical grounds, the concerned employee had crossed the age limit prescribed and thus not eligible

Facts:

The father of the Appellant, an employee of first Respondent, died while in service. He, prior to his death, had already applied for retirement on medical grounds and this application was approved after his death.

Appellant applied for compassionate appointment, which however was rejected on the ground that under the policy on compassionate appointment, in the case of a government servant (falling in Class III and IV), retiring on medical grounds, there is an age limit of 53 years and 55 years respectively which the employee had crossed and this was not the fit case. Hence, the present appeal.

Held, while allowing the appeal:

The above Clause of the policy would have no application in the present case. On the date of death, the application for retirement on medical grounds had not been approved. The approval, which was issued after the death of the employee, would therefore not have any valid basis. There could not have been any retrospective cessation of service by the acceptance of the application of retirement on medical grounds after the date of death of the employee. The case would be covered by Clause 2(a) of the policy which deals with a government servant, who dies while in service leaving the family in immediate need of assistance.

The application of the Appellant to be reconsidered in the light of the above observations and a final decision to be communicated to the Appellant within a period of three months.

FIVE

N.C. SANTHOSH VS. STATE OF KARNATAKA AND ORS., 2020

Hon'ble Judges/Coram:

R. Banumathi, A.S. Bopanna and Hrishikesh Roy, JJ.

Equivalent Citation:

AIR2020SC1401, 2020(2)ESC392(SC), 2020(3)KarLJ400, 2020 (2) KHC 371, 2020(2)KLJ298, (2020)7SCC617, 2020 (5) SCJ 340, 2020(3)SCT512(SC), 2020(2)SLJ155(SC), 2020(3)SLR849(SC), MANU/SC/0277/2020

Relevant sections/provisions: Rules 5 and 9(3) of Karnataka Civil Services Rules, 1996

Number of Pages in the Original Judgment: 6

Case Note:

Service - Compassionate appointment - Denial of - Rules 5 and 9(3) of Karnataka Civil Services Rules, 1996 - Appellants were beneficiary of compassionate appointments, but on discovery that their appointments were made dehors provisions of Karnataka Civil Services Rules, 1996, those appointments came to be cancelled - When their service was terminated aggrieved appointees approached Tribunal - Tribunal found that Appellants were ineligible for appointment under Rules and accordingly dismissed related applications - Aggrieved, writ petitions were filed before High Court which also stand dismissed - Hence, present appeal - Whether appointment of Appellant on compassionate ground, was in violation of Karnataka Civil Services Rules, 1998.

Facts:

The Appellants were the beneficiary of compassionate appointments. But on the discovery that their appointments were made dehors the provisions of the Karnataka Civil Services Rules, 1996 as amended, those appointments came to be cancelled. The amendment to the proviso to Rule 5 stipulated that in case of a minor dependant of the deceased government employee, he/she must apply within one year from the date of death of the government servant and he must have attained the age of eighteen years on the day of making the application. Before amendment, the minor dependant was entitled to apply till one year of attaining majority. When their service was terminated the aggrieved appointees approached the Tribunal. But the Tribunal found that Appellants were ineligible for appointment under the Rules and accordingly dismissed the related applications. The resultant writ petitions were dismissed by the High Court.

Held, while dismissing the appeal:

i. Insofar as the Appellant's claim to legitimacy of appointment on the basis of Rule 9(3) of the Rules, a reading of Rule 9(3) suggests that it is a transitory provision granting extension of time for applying for compassionate appointment. But the transitory provision excludes application filed in contravention of Rule 5, as amended in 1999. In other words, applications filed by minor dependants who had not attained majority within one year from the date of death of the government servants would be in contravention of Rule 5. Therefore, the cases of the Appellants were not covered by the transitory provision of Rule 9(3) introduced by the notification.

i. The norms, prevailing on the date of consideration of the application, should be the basis for consideration of claim for compassionate appointment. A dependent of a government employee, in the absence of any vested right accruing on the death of the government employee, could only demand consideration of his/her application. He was however disentitled to seek consideration in accordance with the norms as applicable, on the day of death of the government employee.

iii. Therefore, this court endorse the Tribunal's view as affirmed by the High Court to the effect that the Appellants were ineligible for compassionate appointment when their applications were considered and the unamended provisions of Rule 5 of the Rules would not apply to them.

ÞÞÞ

SIX

STATE OF MADHYA PRADESH AND ORS. VS. AMIT SHRIVAS, 2020

Hon'ble Judges/Coram:

Sanjay KishanKaul, Aniruddha Bose and Krishna Murari, JJ.

Equivalent Citation:

AIR2020SC4541, 2020(5)ALT276, 2021 1 AWC946SC, 2020(6)BLJ272, 2020(III)CLR358, 2020(2)ESC603(SC), [2021(168)FLR305], 2020(4)JLJ358, 2020LabIC4311, 2020(4)LLN47(SC), 2021(3)MhLj417, 2021(3)MPLJ4, (2020)10SCC496, 2020 (7-8) SCJ 411, 2020(4)SCT505(SC), 2021(1)SLR548(SC), MANU/SC/0726/2020

Relevant sections/provisions: Rule 2(b) of the Madhya Pradesh Civil Service Conduct Rules, 1965

Number of Pages in the Original Judgment: 7

Case Note:

Service - Compassionate appointment - Entitlement thereto - Rule 2(b) of the Madhya Pradesh Civil Service Conduct Rules, 1965 - Claim of compassionate appointment by Respondent (son of deceased employee) - Pension Payment Order issued favouring family basedon last pay-scale and grade pay -Claim of compassionate appointment raised to overcome economic hardship rejected on the basis of existing policy - Writ challenging the rejection allowed by High Court's Single Judge Bench - Writ appeal was dismissed vide impugned judgment - Hence, the present appeal - Whether the Respondent was entitled to receive the benefit of compassionate employment in view of the existing policy.

Facts:

Respondent had raised a claim of entitlement to compassionate appointment after the demise of his father, who was working as a Driver in the Tribal Welfare Department. The claim of the Respondent was predicated on the nature of employment of his late father, who was initially appointed as a work-charged employee. The deceased father had left behind an ailing wife, a son (the Respondent) and three daughters. A Pension Payment Order ('PPO') under the Madhya Pradesh Civil Pension Rules, 1976 was issued in favour of the family on the basis of his last pay-scale and grade pay. In view of the economic hardship faced by family, the Respondent filed an application seeking benefit of compassionate appointment. The Application was rejected on the basis of policy pertaining to a Government servant who dies while in service and was earning a salary from the work-charge/ contingency fund at the time of his/her demise. In such cases, there was no provision for the grant of appointment. Writ challenging the rejection order was allowed by Single Judge Bench of the High Court. The writ appeal filed by Appellant was dismissed with a direction that amount received would be returned. The issue to be determined was whether the Respondent was entitled to receive the benefit of compassionate employment in view of the existing policy.

Held, while allowing the Appeal:

There cannot be any inherent right to compassionate appointment but rather, it is a right based on certain criteria, especially to provide succor to a needy family. This has to be in terms of the applicable policy as existing on the date of demise, unless a subsequent policy is made applicable retrospectively.

No relief, as held could be granted to the Respondent. The family of the late employee has already been paid the entitlement as per applicable policy.

As apparent from the documents on record, a sum of Rs. 1,00,000/- was deposited by the Respondent with the Bank in an interest-bearing deposit in 2016. The FDR was directed to be released to the Respondent and along with interest apart from the additional amount of Rs. 1,00,000/- found payable to the Respondent within a period of two (2) months from order.

The appeal was accordingly allowed.

SEVEN

NATIONAL INSURANCE COMPANY LIMITED VS. BIRENDER AND ORS., 2020

Hon'ble Judges/Coram:

A.M. Khanwilkar and Dinesh Maheshwari, JJ.

Equivalent Citation:

I(2020)ACC130(SC), 2020ACJ759, 2020(207)AIC41, AIR2020SC434, 2020(2)ALD14, 2020 (139) ALR 290, 2020(1) An.W.R. 173(SC), 129(2020)CLT492, 2020(1)J.L.J.R.328, 2020(1)JKJ126[SC], 2020(1)JLJ342, 2020(3)KCCR1641, 2020(2)KLT182, (2020)1MLJ803, 2020(1)PLJR372, 2020(1)RCR(Civil)694, 2020(3)RLW1892(SC), (2020)11SCC356, 2020(1)TAC675, (2020)1WBLR(SC)430, MANU/SC/0028/2020

Relevant Section: Section 166 of Motor Vehicles Act, 1988; Section 2(1) of Arbitration And Conciliation Act, 1996; Section 2(11) of Code of Civil Procedure, 1908 (CPC); Rule 3, Rule 5, Rule 5(1), Rule 5(2), Rule 5(3), Rule 5(4), Rule 5(5) of Haryana Compassionate Assistance to the Dependants of Deceased Government Employees Rules, 2006; Section 140, Section 158(6), Section 165(1), Section 166 and Section 166(1) of Motor Vehicles Act, 1988, Motor Vehicles Act, 1988.

Number of Pages in the Original Judgment: 8

Case Note:

Motor Vehicles - Compensation -Section 166(1) of Motor Vehicles Act, 1988 - Rule 5(2) of Haryana Compassionate Assistance to the Dependants of Deceased Government Employees Rules, 2006 (2006 Rules) - Present appeal was against impugned order of High Court computing compensation on ground that, High Court ought to have deducted the entire amount of financial assistance under the 2006 Rules, instead of deducting only 50% thereof - Whether major sons of deceased who were married and gainfully employed or earning, could claim compensation under Act, 1988 - Whether such legal representatives were entitled only for compensation under conventional heads - Whether amount receivable by legal representatives of deceased under 2006 Rules was required to be deducted as a whole or only portion thereof.

Facts:

The claim petition was filed by the Respondent Nos. 1 and 2 herein, who are the major sons of Smt. Sunheri Devi (deceased). The Respondent Nos. 1 and 2 claimed an amount of Rs. 50,00,000 along with interest at the rate of 12% per annum. The Appellant disputed the claim and pleaded that the accident did not occur with the offending vehicle (the dumper/ tipper) or due to fault of its driver, and that the Respondent Nos. 1 and 2 were majors and not dependant upon the deceased and as such not entitled for any compensation. Further, the vehicle in question was being plied in contravention of terms and conditions of the insurance policy and the driver was not holding a valid and effective driving licence. Resultantly, the insurance company-Appellant was not liable to pay compensation. Tribunal held that the accident of the deceased occurred due to rash and negligent driving of the offending vehicle.

The High Court reduced the compensation awarded by the Tribunal to the extent of Rs.4,84,716 and gave liberty to the Appellant to recover the excess amount, if already paid. The former appeal is preferred by the Appellant on the ground that the High Court ought to have deducted the entire amount of financial assistance under the 2006 Rules, instead of deducting only 50% thereof. The latter appeal has been preferred by the Respondent Nos. 1 and 2, primarily on the ground that the High Court erred in deducting 50% of the amount from compensation instead of one-third (1/ 3rd). Further, deduction of 50% amount of the financial assistance receivable under the 2006 Rules on the assumption that the Respondent Nos. 1 and 2 are eligible therefore is a manifest error.

Held, while allowing the appeal in part:

i. The legal representatives of the deceased could move application for compensation by virtue of Clause (c) of Section 166(1) of Act. The major married son who is also earning and not fully dependant on the deceased, would be still covered by the expression "legal representative" of the deceased. This Court in Manjuri Bera v. The Oriental Insurance Company Ltd. and Anr. Had expounded that liability to pay compensation under the Act does not cease because of absence of dependency of the concerned legal representative. Notably, the expression "legal representative" has not been defined in the Act.
ii. It is thus settled by now that the legal representatives of the deceased have a right to apply for compensation. Even the major married and earning sons of the deceased being legal representatives have a right to apply for compensation and it would be the bounden duty of the Tribunal to consider the application irrespective of the fact whether the concerned legal representative was fully dependant on the deceased and not to limit the claim towards conventional heads only. The evidence on record in the present case would suggest that the claimants were working as agricultural labourers on contract basis and were earning meagre income between Rs. 1,00,000 and Rs. 1,50,000 per annum. In that sense, they were largely dependant on the earning of their mother and in fact, were staying with her, who met with an accident at the young age of 48 years.
iii. The next issue is about the deduction of the amount receivable by the legal representatives of the deceased under the 2006 Rules from the compensation amount determined by the Tribunal in terms of the decision of three-Judge Bench of this Court in Reliance General Insurance Co. Ltd. v. Shashi Sharma.
iv. The view so taken by the High Court is not the correct reading of the decision of three-Judge Bench of this Court in Reliance General Insurance Co. Ltd. v. Shashi Sharma for more than one reason. First, this Court was conscious of the fact that under Rule 5(2) of the 2006 Rules, the family pension receivable by the family would be payable, however, only after the period, during which the financial assistance is received, is completed. In that context, the Court clearly noted that the amount towards family pension cannot be deducted from the claim amount for determination of a just compensation under the Act. Further, the High Court has erroneously assumed that the family of the deceased would be entitled for family pension amount immediately after the death of

the deceased employee. That is in the teeth of the scheme of the 2006 Rules, in particular Rule 5(2) thereof. The said Rules provide for financial assistance on compassionate grounds, as also, other benefits to the family members of the deceased employee and as a package thereof, Rule 5(2) stipulates that the family pension as per the normal Rules would be payable to the family members only after the period of delivery of financial assistance is completed.

v. As a matter of fact, in the present case, the High Court committed manifest error in assuming that the Respondent Nos. 1 and 2 would be eligible to receive financial assistance under the 2006 Rules. The eligibility to receive such financial assistance has been spelt out in Rule 3 of the 2006 Rules read with the provision of Pension/Family Pension Scheme, 1964. It appears that major sons and married daughters are not included in the definition. It has come in the evidence of Gobind Singh, Clerk in SDM Office (PW-1) that the legal representatives of the deceased have not submitted any request for getting financial assistance till he had deposed. Indeed, Respondent No. 1, who had entered the witness box, did depose that they had applied for getting salary of their deceased mother. The fact remains that there is no clear evidence on record that Respondent Nos. 1 and 2 are held to be eligible to get financial assistance or in fact, they are getting such financial assistance under the 2006 Rules. The High Court, therefore, instead of providing for deduction of the amount receivable by the legal representatives of the deceased on this count (under the 2006 Rules), from the compensation amount, should have independently determined the compensation amount and ordered payment thereof subject to legal representatives of the deceased filing affidavit/declaration before the executing Court that they have not received nor would they claim any amount towards financial assistance under the 2006 Rules, so as to become entitled to withdraw the entire compensation amount.

vi. Reverting to the determination of compensation amount, it is noticed that the Tribunal proceeded to determine the compensation amount on the basis of net-salary drawn by the deceased for the relevant period as Rs. 16,918 per month, while taking note of the fact that her gross-salary was Rs. 23,123 per month (presumably below taxable income). Concededly, any deduction from the gross salary other than tax amount cannot be reckoned. In that, the actual salary less tax amount ought to have been taken into consideration by the Tribunal for determining the compensation amount, in light of the dictum of the Constitution Bench of this Court in National Insurance Company Limited v. Pranay Sethi.

vii. Similarly, the High Court despite having taken note of the submission made by the Respondent Nos. 1 and 2 that the deduction for personal expenses of the deceased should be reckoned only as one-third ($1/3^{rd}$) amount for determining loss of dependency, maintained the deduction of 50% towards that head as ordered by the Tribunal. This Court in National Insurance Company Limited v. Pranay Sethi adverted to the dictum of this Court in Sarla Verma (Smt.) and Ors. v. Delhi Transport Corporation and Anr. With approval, wherein it is held that if the dependant family members are 2 to 3, as in this case, the deduction towards personal and living expenses of the deceased should be taken as one-third ($1/3^{rd}$). In other words, the deduction towards personal expenses to the extent of 50% is excessive and not just and proper considering the fact that the Respondent Nos. 1 and 2 alongwith their respective families were staying with the deceased at the relevant time and were largely dependant on her income.

viii. Tribunal, for excluding the amount received by the deceased as family pension due to demise of her husband, had noted that, Learned Counsel for the claimants further requested that about to family pension being drawn by the deceased also be calculated for the purpose of assessing the compensation. This contention and assertion of learned Counsel for the claimants does not carry any conviction with the Tribunal because the deceased was getting family pension in her own right as the widow of the deceased and cannot be termed as her income for the purpose of computing the amount of compensation. The High Court, without reversing the said finding, proceeded to include the amount of Rs. 7,000 per month received by the deceased as pension amount after demise of her husband. Present Court is in agreement with the view taken by the Tribunal and for the same reason, have to reverse the conclusion recorded by the High Court to include the said amount as loss of dependency. That could not have been taken into account, as the same was payable only to the deceased being widow and not her income as such for the purpose of computing the amount of compensation.

ix. Respondent Nos. 1 and 2 would be entitled for compensation to be reckoned on the basis of loss of dependency, due to loss of gross salary (less tax amount, if any) of the deceased and future prospects and deduction of only one-third ($1/3^{rd}$) amount towards personal expenses of the deceased. As regards the multiplier '13' applied by the Tribunal and the High Court, the same needs no interference. As a result, on the facts and in the circumstances of this case, the amount payable towards compensation will have to be recalculated. Loss of dependency due to loss of income calculated at Rs. 31,26,229.60. In addition, the claimants would be entitled for a sum of Rs. 70,000 towards conventional heads in terms of dictum in paragraph 59.8 of Pranay Sethi. Thus, a total sum of Rs.31,96,230 as rounded off, is payable to the claimants. Appeals are partly allowed.

PPP

EIGHT

STATE OF HIMACHAL PRADESH AND ORS. VS. PARKASH CHAND, 2020

Hon'ble Judges/Coram:

Dr. D.Y. Chandrachud and Hemant Gupta, JJ.

Equivalent Citation:

2019(II)CLR900, 2019(1)ESC102(SC), [2019(161)FLR170], 2019(1)J.L.J.R.461, 2019(1)PLJR533, 2019(2)SCALE506, (2019)4SCC285, (2019)1SCC(LS)621, 2019 (6) SCJ 616, 2019(1)SCT646(SC), 2019(1)SLJ1(SC), 2019(3)SLR383(SC), MANU/SC/0076/2019

Relevant Section: Article 226 of Constitution of India

Number of Pages in the Original Judgment: 4

Case Note:

Service - Appointment on compassionate basis - Direction - Validity - Appeal was against direction of High Court and observing that, State should consider cases for appointment on compassionate basis - In case one or more dependants of a deceased-employee was/were in service, though living separately, whether that could be made a ground to deny compassionate appointment to other dependant of deceased-employee.

Facts:

In present matter, father of Respondent who was working as a Peon in Revenue Department of State, died on 4 January 1997, while in service. On date of the death of his father, Respondent was a minor. He attained the age of majority on 17 November 2002. Policy of compassionate appointment framed by State of Himachal Pradesh, contained a stipulation that where none of children of a deceased government employee had attained age of majority at time of death of employee, an application could be submitted on attainment of age of twenty one years by eldest child. This provision was contained in policy dated 18 January 1990. Application submitted by Respondent upon attaining age of majority was processed, but was eventually rejected on ground that, brother of Respondent was already in service of Himachal Pradesh Electricity Board. Fact that, brother of Respondent was employed with a State undertaking was not in dispute. Brother was residing separately for seventeen years was admitted in Writ Petition. Respondent, in reliefs which were sought in petition under Article 226 of Constitution, sought a direction for setting aside letter of rejection dated 25 April 2008 and for his appointment as a Peon on compassionate grounds. High Court had observed that, State should consider cases for appointment on compassionate basis by dealing with the applications submitted by sons, or as the case may be, daughters of deceased government employees, even though, one member of the family was engaged in service of government or an autonomous board or corporation.

Held, while allowing the appeal:

i. Policy contained a stipulation that, where one or more persons of family were already in employment of State Government or of autonomous bodies, Boards, Corporations, etc. of State or Central Government, employment assistance should not be provided to another member of family. However, an exception was carved out in case of widow of deceased government employee, if she claimed that her employed children were not supporting her. Before allowing compassionate appointment, opinion of Department of Personnel and Finance Department was required to be sought and matter was left to ultimate decision of Council of Ministers.
ii. Direction of judgment of High Court virtually amounted to a mandamus to State Government to disregard terms which had been stipulated in paragraph 5(c) of its policy dated 18 January 1990. Policy contained a limited exception which was available only to a widow of a deceased employee who sought compassionate appointment even though one of children of deceased employee was gainfully employed with State. Basis for this exception was to deal with cases where widow was not being supported financially by her children.

iii. In exercise of judicial review under Article 226 of Constitution, it was not open to High Court to re-write terms of policy. It was well-settled that, compassionate appointment was not a matter of right, but must be governed by terms on which State laid down policy of offering employment assistance to a member of family of a deceased government employee.

iv. Judgment of High Court was unsustainable. High Court had virtually re-written terms of policy and had issued a direction to State to consider applications which did not fulfill terms of policy. This was impermissible.

v. Father of Respondent died on 4 January 1997. Though Respondent applied on attaining majority, as permissible under policy, application was rejected on 25 April 2008. Writ Petition was filed nearly two years and six months thereafter. Apart from stating that, elder brother of Respondent who was engaged in government service was living separately, there were no factual averments in support of plea. In any event, High Court was not justified in issuing a direction which would breach policy framed by State.

vi. Directions issued by High Court in its impugned judgment and order was set aside. Appeal allowed.

NINE

State of Himachal Pradesh and Ors. Vs. Shashi Kumar, 2019

Hon'ble Judges/Coram:

Dr. D.Y. Chandrachud and Hemant Gupta, JJ.

Equivalent Citation: 2019(II)CLR875, 2019(1)ESC77(SC), [2019(161)FLR626], 2019(1)J.L.J.R.467, 2019(1)PLJR539, 2019(2)SCALE84, (2019)3SCC653, (2019)1SCC(LS)542, 2019 (6) SCJ 632, 2019(1)SCT707(SC), 2019(1)SLJ133(SC), 2019(3)SLR191(SC), (2019)3WBLR(SC)419, MANU/SC/0081/2019

Relevant Section: Article 226, Articles 14 and Article 16 of the Constitution of India

Number of Pages in the Original Judgment: 14

Ratio Decidendi:

Where family of a deceased employee was not left without means of livelihood, claim for compassionate appointment could not be sustained. Decision was to be taken on a review of overall financial position of family, including amounts received towards terminal benefits.

Case Note:

Service - Compassionate appointment - Direction - Challenge thereto - Present appeal was against order of High Court holding that, State was not entitled to take into account family pension and other terminal benefits in determining whether compassionate appointment should be granted to dependant of a deceased employee - Whether the claim for compassionate appointment had been considered in accordance with the Scheme.

Facts:

Father of Respondent, who was working as HFO in Horticulture Department at Kullu, died on 29 March 2005 while he was in service. On 8 May 2007, Respondent submitted an application for compassionate appointment. Application was forwarded by the Deputy Director, Horticulture at Kullu to competent authorities on 14 September 2007. On 15 January 2008, Additional Secretary (Horticulture) to Government of Himachal Pradesh addressed a communication to Director of Horticulture stating that, income certificate which had been forwarded together with application did not include pension which family was receiving from Government. Accordingly, the Additional Secretary required that a certificate of income, including pension, should be obtained from the concerned SDM by applicant. Writ Petition before High Court was instituted on 11 May 2015, well over seven years thereafter. High Court consolidated a batch of cases, both Letters Patent Appeals and Writ Petitions for hearing. They emanated from a Policy dated 18 January 1990 framed by State Government for providing employment assistance on compassionate grounds to dependants of government servants who had died in harness, leaving a family in need of assistance. High Court held that, State was not entitled to take into account family pension and other terminal benefits in determining whether compassionate appointment should be granted to dependant of a deceased employee. Further, income slab which was prescribed by Finance Department did not constitute an amendment of Policy and that, consequently, it must be disregarded in deciding upon cases of compassionate appointment.

Held, while allowing the appeal:

i. Compassionate appointment was an exception to general Rule that, appointment to any public post in service of State had to be made on basis of principles which accord with Articles 14 and 16 of Constitution. Dependants of a deceased employee of State were made eligible by virtue of Policy on compassionate appointment. Basis of policy was that it recognized that a family of a deceased employee might be placed in a position of financial hardship upon untimely death of employee while in service. It was immediacy of need which furnished basis for State to allow benefit of compassionate appointment. Where authority found that, financial and other circumstances of family were such that in absence of immediate assistance, it would be reduced to being indigent, an application from a dependant member of family could be considered. Terms on which such applications would be considered were subject to policy which was framed by State and must fulfill terms of Policy. It was a well-settled principle of law that, there was no right to compassionate appointment. But, where there was a policy, a dependant member of the family of a deceased employee was entitled to apply for compassionate appointment and to seek consideration of application in accordance with terms and conditions which were prescribed by the State.

ii. Policy in present case which was formulated on 18 January 1990 categorically spoke of providing employment assistance to dependants of government servants who had died while in service, "leaving their families in indigent circumstances". Policy recognized in Paragraph 10 that, benefits which were received by a family on account of welfare measures were required to be considered. Among them, policy stipulated that family pension and death gratuity were required to be taken into account in assessing financial circumstances of family. Policy did not preclude dependants of a deceased employee from being considered for compassionate appointment merely because they were in receipt of family pension. Policy mandated that, receipt of family pension should be taken into account in considering whether family had been left in indigent circumstances requiring immediate means of subsistence. Receipt of family pension was, therefore, one of considerations which was to be taken into account. Paragraph 10(c) of Policy sets out measures provided by State which had a bearing on financial need of family.

iii. In light of recommendations and the Scheme, present Court observed that where family of a deceased employee was not left without means of livelihood, claim for compassionate appointment could not be sustained. In that case, it was on a review of overall financial position of family, including amounts received towards terminal benefits that, decision was taken.

iv. It was in accord with express terms of Scheme of 18 January 1990, as modified by State. Scheme contemplated that payments which had been received on account of welfare measures provided by State including family pension were to be taken into account. Plainly, terms of Scheme must be implemented.

v. Fixation of an income slab was, in fact, a measure which diluted element of arbitrariness. While, undoubtedly, facts of each individual case had to be borne in mind in taking a decision, fixation of an income slab sub-served purpose of bringing objectivity and uniformity in process of decision making. What should be appropriate income criterion was a matter of policy for State Government to determine. Inflation and increase in the cost of living have an important bearing on financial exigencies faced by families of serving as well as deceased employees. In fixing income criteria for considering cases of compassionate appointment, it would be appropriate if State revisited income limit at periodic intervals. It would be open to State to revise income limits at a frequency of less than three years, if State was so advised.

vi. Regarding individual facts pertaining to Respondent were concerned, it had emerged from record that, Writ Petition before High Court was instituted on 11 May 2015. Application for compassionate appointment was submitted on 8 May 2007. On 15 January 2008, Additional Secretary had required that, amount realized by way of pension be included in income statement of family. Respondent waited thereafter for a period in excess of seven years to move a petition under Article 226 of the Constitution. In Umesh Kumar Nagpal, this Court had emphasized that, basis of a scheme of compassionate appointment lies in need of providing immediate assistance to family of deceased employee. This sense of immediacy was evidently lost by the delay on the part of the dependant in seeking compassionate appointment.

vii. Respondent was debarred from seeking compassionate appointment by delay as well as by lapse of time which had taken place.

viii. Writ Petition (CWP No. 3652 of 2015) filed by Respondent before High Court shall stand dismissed and direction of High Court for reconsideration of application for compassionate appointment shall stand set aside. Direction issued by High Court to Appellants to desist from taking into account family pension and other terminal benefits was unsustainable in law and was set aside. Decision of State Government to fix income limits in order to satisfy terms of eligibility for compassionate appointment confirmed. State Government shall, in compliance with Policy, revisit income limits at intervals of three years or earlier and consider whether a revision was warranted having regard to cost of living, inflation and other relevant facts and circumstances. Appeal allowed.

ppp

TEN

STATE OF BIHAR AND ORS. VS. DILIP KUMAR AND ORS., 2019

Hon'ble Judges/Coram:

Dr. D.Y. Chandrachud and Indira Banerjee, JJ.

Equivalent Citation:

2019(5)ALT73, 2019(4)BLJ429, 2019(3)ESC776(SC), 2019(3)J.L.J.R.316, 2019(3)PLJR296, 2019(9)SCALE451, 2019(3)SCT637(SC), 2019(5)SLR290(SC), MANU/SC/0920/2019

Relevant Section: Rule 10 of the Bihar Municipal Body Elementary Teachers (Employment and Service Conditions) Rules, 2006

Number of Pages in the Original Judgment: 5

Case Note:

Service - Grant of compassionate appointment - Direction thereto - Rule 10 of the Bihar Municipal Body Elementary Teachers (Employment and Service Conditions) Rules, 2006 - Appeal was against impugned judgment of Division Bench of High Court affirming view of learned Single Judge and directing grant of compassionate appointment to Respondents on a regular scale of pay in services of the State Government and not on post of Nagar Shikshaks to which they were appointed - Whether High Court erred in directing the Government of Bihar to appoint Respondents in its regular service despite fact that their appointments were made after 2006 Rules were brought into force

Facts:

District Compassionate Appointment Committee considered the request of the Respondents for compassionate appointment. On 12 April 2008, the first Respondent was offered employment on the post of Nagar Shikshak under Rule 10 of Rules, 2006. Second Respondent was offered appointment as a Nagar Shikshak on the basis of the recommendation of the DCAC. Personnel and Administrative Reforms Department of the Government of Bihar, issued an instruction stating that, the posts of Panchayat Teachers and Block Teachers are not borne on the service of the government, hence it is not within the jurisdiction of the DCAC to recommend appointments to those posts. Respondents instituted writ proceedings before the High Court, seeking a mandamus for their appointment on a compassionate basis to posts under the control of the State Government. A learned Single Judge of the High Court accepted the grievance of the Respondents that the posts of Nagar Shikshak to which they were appointed were not government posts with a regular pay scale but were posts with fixed emoluments. This, in the view of the learned Single Judge, was contrary to the Government Instruction dated 17 October 2008. In consequence, while allowing the writ petition, the learned Single Judge directed that the recommendations of the DCAC be implemented "strictly" in accordance with the instruction dated 17 October 2008. Subsequently, on 22 June 2009, the State Government issued a fresh instruction which clarified that it is permissible for the Committee constituted under the Rules to make compassionate appointments to the posts of panchayat teachers/block teachers/town teachers. A Letters Patent Appeal was filed by the state against the decision of the Single Judge. The Division Bench held that since the death of the employees while in service had taken place before the 2006 Rules were enforced, and the circular/ instruction dated 17 October 2008 clarified that, compassionate appointments were required to be made to a post in the service of the government, the writ petition had been correctly allowed. The Division Bench held that the instruction dated 22 June 2009, recalling the earlier circular/instruction, would not take away the effect of the mandamus issued by the Single Judge.

Held, while allowing the appeal:

i. With the enforcement of the 2006 Rules, Rule 10 governs the appointment of Nagar Shikshaks on compassionate grounds. The Respondents were appointed on 12 April 2008 and 19 August 2008, after the enforcement of the 2006 Rules. Their appointments were in terms of

Rule 10 of the 2006 Rules. The Respondents accepted the appointments. The learned Single Judge, in placing reliance on the instruction dated 17 October 2008, failed to notice the 2006 Rules. The Division Bench was of the view that withdrawal of the instruction dated 17 October 2008 by the subsequent instruction dated 22 June 2009 would not obviate compliance with the mandamus issued by the Single Judge on 15 May 2009. The Division Bench ignored the fact that, both the Respondents were appointed in terms of Rule 10 of the 2006 Rules. Having accepted the appointment, it was not open to them to assert, as they did, that they should be appointed in the service of the Government of Bihar. Moreover, no executive instruction could have superseded the rules.

ii. Admittedly, in the present case as well, the Respondents have been appointed after 1 July 2006. Their case would hence be governed by the 2006 Rules. The observations contained in the decision of the Division Bench in Mukesh and Ors. v. State of Bihar and Ors. will apply to the Respondents in the present case. The High Court was manifestly in error in directing the Government of Bihar to appoint the Respondents in its regular service despite the fact that their appointments were made after the 2006 Rules were brought into force. The Respondents duly accepted their appointments as Nagar Shikshaks. However, liberty is granted to the Respondents to approach the State Government for suitable relief. The judgment and order of the High Court is set aside. The civil appeal is allowed.

PPP

ELEVEN

Rajasthan State Road Transport Corporation Vs Danish Khan, 2019

Hon'ble Judges/Coram:

L. Nageswara Rao and Hemant Gupta, JJ.

Equivalent Citation:

AIR2019SC5028, 2019(2) An.W.R. 473(SC), 2019(III)CLR1032, 2020(2)CTC728, 2019(3)ESC798(SC), [2019(163)FLR824], 2020LabIC424, 2020(2)LLN558(SC), 2019(4)RLW2789(SC), 2019(13)SCALE609, (2019)9SCC558, (2019)2SCC(LS)711, 2019 (10) SCJ 299, 2019(4)SCT570(SC), 2020(1)SLJ49(SC), 2020(1)SLR497(SC), 2019(4)TAC353, 2019 (4) WLN 35 (SC), 2020 (1) WLN 1 (SC), MANU/SC/1389/2019

Relevant Section: Regulation 4(3) of Rajasthan State Road Transport Corporation Compassionate Appointment Regulations, 2010

Number of Pages in the Original Judgment: 4

Case Note:

Service - Compassionate appointment - Validity of regulation - Regulation 4(3) of Rajasthan State Road Transport Corporation Compassionate Appointment Regulations, 2010 - Respondent's father who was working as a Helper in Appellant-Corporation died in motor accident - Respondent made representation to Chief Manager of Appellant-Corporation seeking compassionate appointment - Request for compassionate appointment was rejected on ground that Respondent was not entitled in light of Regulation 4(3) of Regulations - Dissatisfied with rejection of request for compassionate appointment, Respondent filed Writ Petition in High Court challenging constitutionality of Regulation 4(3) of Regulations - High Court allowed Writ Petition on ground that Regulation 4(3) of Regulations was discriminatory and violative of Article 14 of Constitution - Hence, present appeal - Whether Regulation 4(3) of Regulations was discriminatory and violative of Article 14 of Constitution.

Facts:

The Respondent's father who was working as a Helper in the Appellant-Corporation died in a motor accident and compensation was awarded to Respondent under Motor Vehicles Act, 1988. The Respondent made a representation to the Chief Manager of the Appellant-Corporation seeking compassionate appointment. The request for compassionate appointment was rejected on the ground that the Respondent was not entitled in light of Regulation 4(3) of the Regulations. Dissatisfied with the rejection of the request for compassionate appointment, the Respondent filed a Writ Petition in the High Court challenging the constitutionality of Regulation 4(3). The High Court allowed the Writ Petition on the ground that Regulation 4(3) of the Regulations was discriminatory and violative of Article 14 of the Constitution.

Held, while allowing the appeal:

i. The Corporation had carved out two classes of dependents of the deceased employees in respect of claims for compassionate appointment. The reason for the disqualification of the dependents of an employee who died in an accident involving the vehicle of the Corporation was to avoid extra burden on the Appellant-Corporation. In such cases, the Appellant-Corporation had to pay the compensation under the Act and also to provide compassionate appointment to the dependents of the deceased employee. In a case where the vehicle of the Appellant-Corporation was not involved in the accident, the compensation under the Act was not the liability of the Appellant-Corporation. It cannot be said that the dependents of an employee who claim both compensation under the Act and compassionate appointment from the Appellant-Corporation were on the same footing as the dependents of the deceased employee whose claim under the Act against a private owner or an insurance company, and compassionate appointment from Appellant-

Corporation.

ii. The two categories of dependents i.e. dependents of employees who had died in an accident while travelling in a vehicle belonging to the Corporation and dependents of the employees who died while travelling in a vehicle not belonging to the Corporation were not similarly situated in respect of their claims against the Corporation. They could not be treated as equals. Therefore, Regulation 4(3) of Regulations could not be said to be discriminatory. Therefore, this court was not in agreement with the judgment passed by the High Court that Regulation 4(3) was violative of Article 14 of the Constitution.

iii. As the Respondent had received the compensation under the Motor Vehicle Act, he was not entitled for compassionate appointment under the Regulations.

TWELVE

STATE BANK OF INDIA AND ORS. VS. SURYA NARAIN TRIPATHI, 2014

Hon'ble Judges/Coram:

H.L. Gokhale and Kurian Joseph, JJ.

Equivalent Citation: 2014(4)ADJ223, 2014(I)CLR1032, (2014)2MLJ494, 2014(3)SCALE536, (2014)15SCC739, 2014(2)SCT161(SC), 2014(II)ShimLC1105, 2015(1)SLJ139(SC), 2014(6)SLR210(SC), (2014)1UPLBEC634, MANU/SC/0173/2014

Relevant Section: Article 16 of the Constitution of India

Number of Pages in the Original Judgment: 03

Case Note:

Service - Compassionate ground - Validity thereof - Present appeal filed against order whereby Respondent was appointed on compassionate ground - Whether impugned order of appointment on compassionate ground was liable to be set aside- Held, if employer points out that financial arrangement made for family subsequent to death of employee was adequate, members of family could not insist that one of them ought to be provided comparable appointment - Respondent was not justified in contending that Appellant-Bank should provide appointment to one of members of family when main bread earner had passed away - Appellant-Bank had made appropriate financial provision at par with similar arrangement - Therefore it was not possible to say that Court could have directed Bank to consider compassionate appointment - Impugned order of appointment on compassionate ground was set aside - Appeal allowed.

Brief Facts:

i. The brief facts of this appeal are that the one B.P. Tripathi the father of the first Respondent was working in the State Bank of India from 27.12.1969 and he died while in service on 19.1.1998 after completing more than 28 years of service. At that time he was working as Assistant Manager. The Respondent No. 1 who is his son applied for a job on compassionate basis and his application was turned down by the Bank which led to the writ petition. The writ petition was allowed by the learned Single Judge and the appeal of the Bank there from was dismissed. Hence this appeal by special leave.

ii. It is submitted by Mr. Vikas Singh learned senior counsel appearing for Appellants that earlier in the year 1979 there was a different scheme which was prevalent in the matter of compassionate appointment, and amongst others there was a provision for an interview under Clause 7.5(f) of the Hand Book on Staff Matters. In 1994 this Court rendered a judgment in Umesh Kumar Nagpal v. State of Haryana and Ors. reported in MANU/SC/0701/1994 : 1994 (4) SCC 138 wherein it was laid down that the object of compassionate appointment is meant to enable the bereaved family of the deceased employee to face the sudden financial crisis and not to provide employment as such. This led the Bank to frame another policy in the year 1998. This judgment is referred in the new policy and it is provided therein as an objective that when the Bank is satisfied that the financial condition of the family is such that it requires employment that compassionate appointment will be offered.

iii. It is the case of the Bank that as far as the present appointment is concerned all relevant factors were considered. It was noticed that the salary of the deceased at the time of his death was Rs. 8,970/-. His family was given an amount of Rs. 5,98,092/- plus 0.25 lakh as terminal benefits. If the said amount was to be invested properly, it would get interest at least of Rs. 5,000/- p.m. This was apart from the family pension of Rs. 4208+Admissible D.A. The Bank, therefore, took the view that the circumstances do not warrant the compassionate appointment for the Respondent which was applied for.

Held, while allowing the petition:

i. In all the matters of compassionate appointment it must be noticed that it is basically a way out for the family which is financially in difficulties on account of the death of the bread earner. It is not an avenue for a regular employment as such. This is in fact an exception to the provisions under Article 16 of the Constitution. That being so, if an employer points out that the financial arrangement made for the family subsequent to the death of the employee is adequate, the members of the family cannot insist that one of them ought to be provided a comparable appointment. This being the principle which has been adopted all throughout, it is difficult for us to accept the submission made on behalf of the Respondent.

ii. As stated earlier, the deceased left behind a large family. The fact however, remains that by now 15 years have gone since then. Besides the Bank has made appropriate financial provision at par with similar arrangement that was noted by this Court in the case of M.T. Latheesh (supra). Therefore it is not possible for us to say that the Court could have directed the Bank to consider compassionate appointment. In the circumstances, the appeal is allowed. The judgment rendered by the learned Single Judge as well as by the Division Bench are set aside. The writ petition No. 5045 of 1999 filed by the Respondent shall stand dismissed.

iii. Although we are allowing this appeal, Mr. Vikas Singh very fairly stated that looking at the difficulties of the family, and that the Respondent was required to go through the litigation upto the Supreme Court, the Court may consider granting appropriate litigation expenses to the Respondent. We quite appreciate this gesture and order that the Appellant Bank will pay an amount of Rs. 1 lakh to the Respondent on this count. However, we make it clear that this order on costs is made in consideration of the special facts of this case.

THIRTEEN

State of Gujarat and Ors. Vs. Arvind Kumar T. Tiwari and Ors., 2012

Hon'ble Judges/Coram:

B.S. Chauhan and F.M. Ibrahim Kalifulla, JJ.

Equivalent Citation: AIR2012SC3281, 2012(4)BLJ119, 2013(2)B.L.J.330, 2013(1)CLJ(SC)48, 2012(III)CLR418, 2012(4)ESC580(SC), JT2012(11)SC521, 2012(4)KLJ98, 2012LabIC3977, 2013(1)MhLj555, 2013(1)MhLJ555(SC), 2013MPLJ256(SC), 2012(8)SCALE664, (2012)9SCC545, [2012]7SCR1072, 2013(1)SCT117(SC), 2013(2)SLJ11(SC), 2013(1)SLR1(SC), (2013)1WBLR(SC)81, MANU/SC/0742/2012

Relevant Section: Articles 14 and 16 of Constitution of India

Number of Pages in the Original Judgment: 05

Ratio Decidendi:

"Compassionate appointment cannot be claimed as a matter of right."

Case Note:

Service - Compassionate appointment - Respondent No. 1 filed application for employment in police department on compassionate ground, for post of peon - Said application was rejected on ground that family of deceased was not suffering from any financial constraints and was getting adequate amount of pension over and above income limit fixed by Government for this purpose - Application was directed to be reconsidered but was again rejected on ground that he did not meet minimum eligibility requirement for said post, as he had not passed 10th standard, which was a necessary pre-requisite for consideration for post on compassionate ground as per Notification issued in 2005 - However in Special Civil Application, Court held that, as said employee had died in year 1999, amended provision would not apply to his case, therefore direction was issued to consider Respondent's case without being influenced by earlier order, in light of new policy/circular/rules - Division Bench, rejected Appellant's Appeal - Hence, this Appeal - Whether, High Court erred in observing that new policy/rules did not apply retrospectively, and that case of Respondent No. 1 should be considered in light of existing rules, i.e., rules which were in force prior to 2005 - Held, it was a settled legal proposition that compassionate appointment could not be claimed as a matter of right - It was not simply another method of recruitment - A claim to be appointed on such a ground, has to be considered in accordance with Rules, Regulations or administrative instructions governing subject, taking into consideration financial condition of family of deceased - However Clause 9, provides that no relaxation in educational qualification(s) for purpose of giving compassionate appointment to dependant(s) of a deceased employee, would be permissible - However such relaxation could be granted if there exists some requirement of minimum qualification(s) with respect to said post - Clause 11, provides that a dependant could be given appointment on compassionate ground, on basis of pass marks obtained by him in new Secondary School Certificate and in view thereof, as Respondent No. 1 was admittedly only 8th standard (fail), he was therefore, ineligible for post - Since 1991 itself, eligibility criteria for a Class IV post was set as passing of 10th standard and as said Respondent had been unable to pass even 8th standard, he was not eligible to apply for said post - Hence judgment and order impugned was set aside - Appeal allowed.

Brief Facts:

i. The father of Respondent No. 1 who was working in the Police Department, State of Gujarat as the Assistant Sub-Inspector of Police, died in harness on 9.4.1999. Immediately thereafter, Respondent No. 1 filed an application for employment on compassionate ground, for the post of Peon. As he had completed his education only upto the 8th standard, the said application was rejected vide order dated 13.10.2000, on the ground that the family of the deceased was not suffering from any financial constraints and was getting an adequate amount of pension, which was, in fact, over and above the income limit fixed by the Government for this purpose. The said application was considered by the Additional Director General of Police by way of passing order dated 23.6.2003, directing that the application of Respondent No. 1 be reconsidered, ignoring the abovementioned issue regarding financial condition. The said application was rejected vide order dated 3.7.2005, on the ground that the applicant did not meet the minimum eligibility requirement for the said post, as he had not passed the 10th standard, which was a necessary pre-requisite for the consideration of the application of Respondent No. 1 for a Class IV post on compassionate ground.

ii. Aggrieved, Respondent No. 1 preferred Special Civil Application No. 5630/ 2007, which was disposed of vide judgment and order dated 2.3.2007, considering the fact that there was a subsequent notification dated 16.3.2005, which provided for the minimum qualification requirement of 10th standard pass, as the eligibility criteria for employment to a Class IV post. However, it was held that, as the said employee had died in the year 1999, the amended provision would not apply to his case. Therefore, direction was issued to consider his case without being influenced by the earlier order, in light of the new policy/circular/rules.

iii. Aggrieved, the said order was challenged before the Division Bench, by the Appellant, which was rejected vide impugned judgment and order dated 4.2.2008. Hence, this appeal.

Held, while allowing the petition:

i. In view of the above, we are of the considered opinion that since 1991, the eligibility criteria for a Class IV post was set as, the passing of the 10th standard, and as the said Respondent had been unable to pass even the 8th standard, he was most certainly, not eligible to apply for the said post. In view of the law referred to hereinabove, it is neither desirable, nor permissible in law, for this Court to issue direction to relax the said eligibility criteria and appoint Respondent No. 1 merely on humanitarian grounds.

ii. Thus, the question framed by this Court with respect to whether the application for compassionate employment is to be considered as per existing rules, or under the rules as existing on the date of death of the employee, is not required to be considered.

iii. In view of the above, the appeal succeeds and is allowed. The judgment and order impugned herein is set aside. No order as to costs.

FOURTEEN

Bhawani Prasad Sonkar Vs. Union of India (UOI) and Ors., 2011

Hon'ble Judges/Coram:

Devinder Kumar Jain and H.L. Dattu, JJ.

Equivalent Citation: 2011(2)CLJ(SC)68, 2011(I)CLR1002, JT2011(3)SC293, 2011(3)KCCRSN247, 2011LabIC1848, 2011-3-LW142, 2011(3)SCALE513, (2011)4SCC209, (2011)1SCC(LS)667, [2011]4SCR630, 2011(2)SLJ44(SC), 2011(3)SLR225(SC), MANU/SC/0242/2011

Relevant Section: Persons with Disabilities (Equal Opportunities, Protection of Rights and Full Participation) Act, 1995

Number of Pages in the Original Judgment: 06

Case Note:

Service - Compassionate Appointment - High Court dismissed Petition seeking compassionate appointment on ground that appellant did not fulfill conditions envisaged in Railway Board Circular dated 29th November, 2001 - Challenge against thereto - Hence the present Appeal - Held, Appellant's father was not offered any alternative employment in terms of Circular dated 29th April, 1999 but was retired from service pursuant to recommendation of Standing Committee - Having denied Appellant's father benefit of Circular of 29th April 1999, Respondents cannot claim that Circular of November, 2001 was applicable to Appellant's father, disentitling him from seeking employment on compassionate ground for his son as he was not totally incapacitated and had sought voluntary retirement - Hence, earlier circular dated 22nd September, 1995 applicable in instant case entitling appellant to employment on compassionate ground as said circular contemplates compassionate employment for wards of those employees who have been medically de-categorized and have retired without being offered alternative suitable job - Appeal allowed Service - Compassionate Employment - Guidelines - Compassionate employment given solely on humanitarian grounds and same could not be claimed as matter of right - Such employment not made in absence of rules or regulations issued by Government or public authority - Request considered strictly in accordance with governing scheme and no discretion left with authority to make compassionate appointment dehors the scheme - An appointment on compassionate ground meets sudden crisis occurring in family on account of death or medical invalidation of employee while in service - Such employment permissible only to one dependant of deceased/ incapacitated employee only in lowest category viz., Class III and IV posts

Brief Facts:

i. This appeal, by grant of special leave, is directed against the judgment dated 1st September, 2003 delivered by the High Court of Judicature at Allahabad at Lucknow, whereby the writ petition filed by the Appellant herein, seeking compassionate appointment, has been dismissed on the ground that he did not fulfil the conditions envisaged in the Railway Board Circular dated 29th November, 2001.

ii. Appellant's father, Mr. Prahladji Sonkar, was posted as a Guard Mail/ Express, North Eastern Railway at the Lucknow Junction. Respondent No. 2 viz. the Senior Divisional Karmik Adhikari, North Eastern Railway (N.E.R.), Lucknow directed the Appellant's father to appear before the Medical Board for a medical examination. Accordingly, Appellant's father appeared before the Medical Board and was declared medically unfit in A2, A3, B1 and B2 categories vide certificate dated 6th March, 1998. However, he was found fit in C1 and C2 categories and was directed to appear for another medical examination after six months.

iii. Accordingly, Appellant's father again appeared for a medical examination and vide certificate dated 13th July, 1999, he was declared medically unfit as de-categorized employee. Nevertheless, he was found fit in category B1 and below. Thereafter, on 9th August, 1999, Appellant's father appeared before the Standing Committee which decided to retire him without offering him any alternate employment, as stipulated in the service rules. Ultimately, Appellant's father was retired from service vide retirement order dated 30th August, 1999 issued by Respondent No. 3 viz. Divisional Railways Manager (Karmik), Lucknow, which stated that:

iv. Shri Prahlad Ji Sonkar, Guard Mail/Express in the pay scale of (5500-9000) at Lucknow Junction who having been declared as decategorised employee has been recommended by the standing committee for retirement, is retired with immediate effect.

Held, while allowing the appeal:

i. In light of the fact that Circular dated 29th November, 2001 was not applicable in the case of Appellant's father, inasmuch as the benefit of the 29th April, 1999 Circular was not extended to him, and he was made to retire from service, we are of the opinion that the earlier circular dated 22nd September, 1995 is applicable in the instant case. Consequently, the Appellant would be entitled to employment on compassionate ground as the said Circular contemplates compassionate employment for the wards of those employees who have been medically de-categorized, and have retired, without being offered an alternative suitable job. We are unable to accept the plea of the Respondents that on being de-categorized, Appellant's father had opted for voluntary retirement.

ii. In light of the foregoing discussion, the appeal is allowed; the impugned judgment is set aside and it is directed that the Appellant shall be granted employment on compassionate ground within three months of the receipt of copy of this judgment, subject to his complying with other eligibility conditions, as applicable on 1st September, 1999. However, for all intents and purposes, he shall be deemed to be in service from the date of actual joining.

iii. In the facts and circumstances of the case, there shall be no order as to costs.

PPP

FIFTEEN

Mumtaz Yunus Mulani Vs. State of Maharashtra and Ors., 2008

Hon'ble Judges/Coram:

S.B. Sinha and V.S. Sirpurkar, JJ.

Equivalent Citation: 2008(67)AIC129, 2009(1)ALT14(SC), 2008(2)ESC273(SC), [2008(117)FLR565], JT2008(4)SC512, 2008LabIC3580, 2008(4)SCALE637, (2008)11SCC384, (2008)2SCC(LS)1077, 2008(2)SCT669(SC), 2008(3)SLJ433(SC), 2008(3)SLR782(SC), (2008)2UPLBEC1494, MANU/SC/7338/2008

Relevant Section: Article 14 of the Constitution of India.

Number of Pages in the Original Judgment: 05

Ratio Decidendi:

Appointment on compassionate ground is not a source of recruitment.

Case Note:

Service - Appointment - Compassionate - Appellant's husband working in a public charitable trust expired - Filed an application for appointment on compassionate ground - Denied on the ground of payment of family pension - Family pension received was Rs. 1,100 - Writ petition filed before the High Court was dismissed - Whether compassionate appointment of the appellant is warranted - Held, appointment on compassionate ground can only be granted to tide over the sudden crisis of the family of the deceased

- Not a source of recruitment - Scheme which was operative at the relevant point of time was that appointment on compassionate ground should not be given if the monthly income exceeds Rs. 500 - Appeal dismissed.

Brief Facts:

i. Appellant is the widow of one Yunus Dastagir Mulani. He was a Peon witking in the respondent, a vocational institution. It is a public charitable trust. Appellant's husband expired on 6.9.1996. She filed an application for appointment on compassionate ground. As no response thereto was received, she made representations. Second Respondent, however, declined to give any appointment on compassionate ground to the appellant. She filed a writ petition before the High Court. By reason of the impugned judgment the said petition has been dismissed.

ii. Mr. Makarand D. Adkar, learned Counsel appearing on behalf of the appellant, would submit that the reason for depriving the appellant of the right to be appointed on compassionate ground, being payment of family pension, the impugned judgment cannot be sustained. It was contended that the appellant has a large family to maintain which includes her two grown up children. The family pension received by her being only Rs. 1,100/- per month, the respondent should be directed to offer appointment on compassionate ground to her even at that stage.

iii. Learned Counsel appearing on behalf of the respondents, on the other hand, would contend that immediately upon the death of the appellant's husband, the respondents supported the case of the appellant in assisting her to get the retrial benefits of her husband. However, in the year 1997, another person being Mr. Arun Uttereshwar having been appointed, it is not possible to dismiss him from service so as to accommodate the appellant.

iv. Appellant's husband was appointed in a Class IV post. The school is an aided institution. The State, although instructed the respondent to appoint the appellant on compassionate ground, it appears, such an instruction had been issued in view of the scheme for appointment on compassionate ground as contained in the Government Order dated 31st December, 2002. The said resolution, inter alia, reads as under:

a. Regarding giving appointment on compassionate principle, the above scheme will be applicable to all teachers and employees other than teachers of private, primary, secondary and higher middle as well as training schools for teachers.

b. Rules relating to absorption of relatives of employees deceased or retired because of medical reason, are given in the enclosed Annexure "A".
c. Information about application to be made for service by the concerned relatives of employees and documents to be submitted along with it will be as mentioned in Annexure "B".
d. If the decision is taken prior to implementation of this scheme in respect of giving/refusing to give appointment on compassionate principle, those cases should not be taken into consideration for review. However, those employees who are deceased or those employees who are prematurely retired because of incurable illness after 1 January, 2001, in case if persons from such family have applied for appointment on compassionate principle, and if in case their application has been turned down, such relatives can submit their application again afresh in this scheme.

Held, while dismissing the appeal:

i. We may also observe that when the Division Bench of the High Court was considering the case of the applicant holding that he had sought "compassion", the Bench ought to have considered the larger issue as well and it is that such an appointment is an exception to the general rule. Normally, an employment in the Government or other public sectors should be open to all eligible candidates who can come forward to apply and compete with each other. It is in consonance with Article 14 of the Constitution. On the basis of competitive merits, an appointment should be made to public office. This general rule should not be departed from except where compelling circumstances demand, such as, death of the sole breadwinner and likelihood of the family suffering because of the setback. Once it is proved that in spite of the death of the breadwinner, the family survived and substantial period is over, there is no necessity to say "goodbye" to the normal rule of appointment and to show favour to one at the cost of the interests of several others ignoring the mandate of Article 14 of the Constitution.
ii. In this case, the respondent is a charitable institution. It is run on Government aid. It cannot afford to appoint persons in a post which has not been sanctioned. It has not been denied or disputed that one Arun Uttareshwar has already been appointed in place of the deceased

husband of the appellant. It does not matter as to whether the said appointment has been approved by the State or not inasmuch as if it had not been done, on the basis of the policy decision contained its is resolution dated 31st December 2002 the same cannot be considered to be of much significance, particularly, in view of the fact that the appellant's husband died as far back as on 16.9.1996 and the vacancy had been filled up in the year 1997.

iii. Furthermore, about 12 years have passed. Appellant's son is aged about 20 years and daughter is aged about 16 years. Therefore, they have become major. Appellant herself would be aged about 38 years now. She cannot be given any appointment at this age.

Keeping in view the fact situation obtaining in this case, we are of the opinion that no case has been made out for exercising our discretionary jurisdiction under Article 136 of the Constitution of India. This appeal, therefore, is dismissed. No costs

PPP

SIXTEEN

General Manager, State Bank of India and Ors. Vs. Anju Jain, 2008

Hon'ble Judges/Coram:

C.K. Thakker and Devinder Kumar Jain, JJ.

Equivalent Citation: 2008(6)ALLMR(SC)442, 2009(4)ALT3(SC), 2008(56)BLJR2842, 2008(4)ESC606(SC), [2008(119)FLR714], JT2008(9)SC272, 2008LabIC3616, (2009)ILLJ319SC, 2009-2-LW344, 2009(2)MhLj41, (2008)7MLJ895(SC), 2009MPLJ1(SC), RLW2008(4)SC3244, 2008(11)SCALE647, (2008)8SCC475, 2008(4)SCT305(SC), 2009(1)SLJ83(SC), 2009(1)SLR463(SC), 2009(1)SLR463(SC), 2008(2)UJ1040, MANU/SC/3729/2008

Relevant Section: Article 226 of the Constitution of India.

Number of Pages in the Original Judgment: 06

Ratio Decidendi:

"If during the carrier of the employee, he had committed illegalities and the misconduct is proved and he is punished, his dependents cannot claim right to compassionate appointment."

Case Note:

Service - Compassionate appointment - Rejection of - Husband of the Writ Petitioner died while in service in the Appellant Bank - Before death, a major punishment was imposed on him on charges of gross misconduct of embezzlement/ misappropriation - Writ-Petitioner applied to the Bank for compassionate appointment - Prayer rejected - On appeal, the Single Judge of the High Court held that right, which had accrued in her favour, could not be taken away by the Bank only on the ground of misconduct on the part of her husband for which he was punished - High Court directed the Bank to provide her appointment on compassionate ground, which was upheld by the Division Bench - Hence, the present appeal - Appellant contended that dependent of a employee who has committed misconduct for which he was punished, cannot claim the benefit of appointment on compassionate ground - Whether dependent of an employee who had died or retired on medical ground but whose service record was blemished on account of disciplinary action can be a ground for denial compassionate appointment in the Bank - Held, appointment on compassionate ground is never considered a right of a person - It is really a concession in favour of dependents of deceased employee - If during the carrier of the employee, he had committed illegalities and the misconduct is proved and he is punished, his dependents cannot claim right to the employment - In the present case, Bank was governed by the scheme under which the dependent of an employee who had died or retired on medical ground but whose service record was blemished on account of disciplinary action having been taken against him will not be considered eligible for compassionate appointment in the Bank - Bank right in refusing appointment on compassionate ground - Impugned Judgments set aside - Appeals allowed.

Brief Facts:

i. The present appeal is filed by the General Manager, State Bank of India ('the State Bank' for short) and others against judgment and order passed by a Single Judge of the High Court of Judicature at Allahabad on March 2, 2006 in C.M.W.P. No. 45006 of 2001 and confirmed by the Division Bench of the said Court on April 25, 2007 in Special Appeal No. 390 of 2006. By the said order, the High Court allowed the petition filed by Smt. Anju Jain, writ-petitioner (respondent herein) and directed the State Bank to provide her appointment on compassionate ground on the death of her husband.

ii. Shortly stated the facts of the case are that Mr. Jain, husband of the respondent- writ petitioner was working as Assistant with the State Bank at Karhall Branch, Agra in the State of U.P. In September, 1995, he was placed under suspension and charge-sheeted for having committed gross misconduct of embezzlement/ misappropriation. Departmental inquiry was instituted against him wherein he was found guilty. In 1996, on the basis of findings recorded by the Inquiry Officer and accepted by the Disciplinary Authority, major punishment was imposed on him by which his basic pay was reduced by two stages and five annual future increments were also stopped with cumulative effect. Husband of the writ-petitioner, however, died on January 25, 2000 while in service in the State Bank.

iii. The State Bank had framed a scheme for appointment on compassionate grounds for dependents of deceased employees/employees retired on medical grounds with effect from January 01, 1979. It was modified from time to time. At the relevant time, when the husband of the writ-petitioner died (January 25, 2000), the policy as amended with effect from January 01, 1998 was in force.

iv. In accordance with the policy of giving employment on compassionate ground to dependents of a deceased employee, the writ- petitioner, as the widow of the deceased applied to the State Bank in March, 2000. The competent authority of the Bank considered the case of the writ petitioner and keeping in view the punishment imposed on the deceased employee, it rejected the prayer of the writ petitioner and informed her that no such appointment could be given to her. A representation was made by the writ petitioner but it was also rejected on July 16, 2001.

Held, while dismissing the appeal:

i. Apart from the fact that in 'peculiar circumstances', a positive direction was issued by this Court and it was stated that the decision 'is no precedent' with respect to the subject, in our opinion, in the present case, the second stage did not arise at all. As we have held that even under the policy in force in 2000, the appellant Bank was wholly right and fully justified in declining the prayer of the widow of deceased employee in rejecting her prayer for extending benefit of appointment on compassionate ground. The orders passed by both the Courts are, therefore, liable to be set aside on that ground alone.

ii. For the aforesaid reasons, the appeal is allowed, the order passed by the Single Judge and confirmed by the Division Bench of the High Court is set aside and the writ petition filed by the widow of deceased employee of the State Bank for getting an appointment as dependent of deceased employee on compassionate ground is ordered to be dismissed.

iii. On the facts and in the circumstances of the case, however, the parties are ordered to bear their own costs.

SEVENTEEN

The Secretary, A.P. Social Welfare-Residential Educational Institutions Vs. Pindiga Sridhar and Ors., 2007

Hon'ble Judges/Coram:

H.K. Sema and Devinder Kumar Jain, JJ.

Equivalent Citation: AIR2007SC1527, 2007(3)ALLMR(SC)336, 2007(5)ALT29(SC), 2007 (3) AWC 2295 (SC), [2007(113)FLR465], (2007)3MLJ870(SC), 2007(4)SCALE479, (2007)13SCC352, (2008)2SCC(LS)656, [2007]4SCR145, 2007(2)SCT585(SC), 2008(3)SLJ169(SC), 2007(3)SLR893(SC), 2007(1)UJ486, MANU/SC/1477/2007

Relevant Section: Article 14 and 16 of the Constitution of India

Number of Pages in the Original Judgment: 03

Ratio Decidendi:

"Prior show cause notice not called for terminating appointment secured on compassionate ground by playing fraud."

Case Note:

i. Constitution of India - Articles 14 and 16-Employment-Principles of natural justice-Appointment on compassionate ground-Father of first respondent died-in-harness on 31.3.1996 - He applied for compassionate appointment on 6.5.1996-His mother already employed as teacher-He did not disclose this fact in his application-His wife also appointed as Extension Officer on 3.8.1997-He obtained compassionate appointment as typist on 22.11.2002 - But his appointment terminated on 15.3.2003 on ground that he secured appointment by suppressing facts - Whether termination justified?-Held, "yes"-Appointment obtained by him by playing fraud-Whether termination vitiated for non-observance of principles of natural justice?-Held, "no"-No prejudice caused to respondent-He could not have improved his case even if S.C.N. issued to him-View of High Court clearly erroneous - Impugned judgment of D.B. set aside.

ii. Constitution of India-Article 14-Principles of natural justice-Complaint of violation-Cannot be sustained unless prejudice established to have been caused by violation.

Brief Facts:

i. The father of the respondent late Sri P. Andhru was employed in the Government of Andhra Pradesh as a Hostel Warden. He died in harness on 31.3.1996. The respondent being one of the sons of late Sri P. Andhru applied for appointment on compassionate ground by his application dated 6.5.1996. He was appointed as a typist on 22.11.2002 on compassionate ground. His appointment on compassionate ground came to be terminated by an order dated 15.3.2003 on the ground that he secured the appointment by suppressing the facts. He unsuccessfully challenged the order of termination before the learned Single Judge. However, on appeal being preferred by him the Division Bench of the High Court upset the well-merited order of the learned Single Judge, on the sole ground that the order of termination violates the principles of natural justice as no show cause notice has been given to the respondent before the impugned order was issued. Hence the present appeal by special leave.

ii. The undisputed facts are:

Late Sri P. Andhru was survived by wife Smt. P. Santhoshamma and two sons namely Sri P. Sridhar (respondent herein) and Sri P. Srikanth. At the time when the respondent made an application for appointment on compassionate ground, the mother of the respondent (Smt. P. Santhoshamma) was employed as a teacher in Z.P. High School, Suryapet. The wife of the respondent Sirisha was appointed as Extension Officer in the Rural Development on 3.8.1997 and later on, she was promoted as Mandal Parishad Development Officer. The respondent as earlier noticed was appointed as a typist on compassionate ground on 22.11.2002. The aforesaid fact was conceded by the counsel appearing for the respondent. The fact, therefore, reveals that when he made an application for appointment on compassionate ground on 6.5.1996, the mother of the respondent was employed as a teacher in Z.P. High School, Suryapet, which fact was not disclosed by him in his application dated 6.5.1996. It is also clear that the wife of the respondent was in service as a Mandal Parishad Development Officer, when the respondent was appointed as a typist on compassionate ground on 22.11.2002.

Held, while allowing the appeal:

i. The High Court on the basis of the erroneous view upset the well-merited judgment of the learned Single Judge. By now, it is well settled principle of law that the principles of natural justice cannot be applied in a straight jacket formula. Its application depends upon the facts and circumstances of each case. To sustain the complaint of the violation of principles of natural justice one must establish that he was prejudiced for non-observance of the principles of natural justice. In the present case, the fact on which the appellant terminated the services of the respondent appointed on compassionate ground was admitted by the respondent himself that when he applied for the post on compassionate ground by its application dated 6.5.1996, his mother was in service. So also when he secured the appointment by an order dated 22.11.2002 his wife was in service since 3.8.1997 as Extension Officer in Rural Development and later on promoted as Mandal Parishad Development Officer at the time when he was appointed on compassionate ground. These facts clearly disclose that the appointment on compassionate ground was secured by playing fraud. Fraud clocks everything. In such admitted facts, there was no necessity of issuing show cause notice to him. The view of the High Court that termination suffers from the non-observance of the principles of natural justice is, therefore, clearly erroneous. In our view, in the given facts of this case, no prejudice whatsoever has been caused to the respondent. The respondent could not have improved his case even if a show cause notice was issued to him.

ii. In the result, the order of the Division bench of the High Court dated 23.8.2005, is accordingly set aside. The appeal is allowed. The order of the learned Single Judge is restored and writ petition of the respondent stands dismissed. No costs.

EIGHTEEN

I.G. (KARMIK) AND ORS. VS. PRAHALAD MANI TRIPATHI, 2007

Hon'ble Judges/Coram:

S.B. Sinha and Markandey Katju, JJ.

Equivalent Citation: 2007(4)ADJ661, 2007(3)ALLMR(SC)866, 2007(5)ALT12(SC), 2008(1)ESC107(SC), [2007(114)FLR9], JT2007(7)SC556, 2007(6)SCALE370, (2007)6SCC162, (2007)2SCC(LS)417, [2007]5SCR978, 2007(3)SCT483(SC), 2008(1)SLJ89(SC), 2007(4)SLR595(SC), (2008)1UPLBEC35, MANU/SC/7340/2007

Relevant Section: Article 16 of the Constitution of India

Number of Pages in the Original Judgment: 04

Ratio Decidendi:

"Appointment - Compassionate Grounds - A person cannot be appointed unless he fulfills the eligibility criteria which is applicable even in cases of appointment on compassionate grounds"

Case Note:

i. Employment - Appointment on compassionate ground-Father of respondent died in harness as Police constable-Respondent not found fit for appointment as constable-Hence, appointed on compassionate ground as peon-He accepted appointment-Whether he can be permitted subsequently to turn round and contend that he was entitled to higher post-Impugned judgment unsustainable and set aside.

ii. Employment - Compassionate appointment-It is given only for meeting immediate hardship faced by family because of death of bread earner.
iii. Employment - Appointment on compassionate ground-Once right to such appointment consummated-Any further or second consideration for higher post on ground of compassion would not arise.

Brief Facts:

i. Respondent's father Shri Narmadeshwar Mani Tripathi was a constable. He was in Uttar Pradesh Police Service. He died in harness on 2.1.1986. Grant of appointment to a dependant of an employee who died in harness is governed by statutory rules, in terms whereof the appellant filed an application for his appointment. He disclosed his academic qualification therein. He was considered for appointment as a Constable. He was not found eligible therefore having not satisfied the physical standard stipulated under the rules. He was appointed as a Peon. He accepted the said appointment without any demur whatsoever. He, however filed an application before the Uttar Pradesh Services Tribunal, Lucknow praying for his absorption in the post of Constable (M) with consequential benefits from the date of his initial appointment. By reason of a Judgment and Order dated 24.7.2000, the Tribunal arrived at a finding that although, ordinarily, rule of estoppel apply in a case of this nature, having regard to the representations made by him before the authorities in the instant case, the same should not be applied. It directed the appellant to appoint him in Class III posts with a further direction that the services rendered by him in the post of ordinary Peon be counted towards his pensionary benefits in the class III posts.
ii. A Writ Petition was filed before the High Court questioning the correctness of said order. By reason of the impugned judgment dated 27.11.2002, the High Court declined to interfere therewith despite observing;

A word of caution, is put on record that the right to claim appointment under the dying in harness rules on compassionate ground can be neither used as a devise to seek employment nor it is a new mode of recruitment in Government service nor can be treated as a channel of promotion to higher post. The impugned order has been passed on the basis of facts of the present case.

Held, while allowing the appeal:

Appellant accepted the said post without any demur whatsoever. He, therefore, upon obtaining appointment in a lower post could not have been permitted to turn round and contend that he was entitled for a higher post although not eligible therefore. A person cannot be appointed unless he fulfils the eligibility criteria. Physical fitness being an essential eligibility criteria, the Superintendent of Police could not have made any recommendation in violation of the rules. Nothing has been shown before us that even the petitioner came within the purview of any provisions containing grant of relaxation of such qualification. Whenever, a person invokes such a provision, it would be for him to show that the authority is vested with such a power.

The pre-requisite for making such a appointment by granting relaxation has been laid down by this Court in Indian Drugs & Pharmaceuticals Ltd. v. Devki Devi and Ors. MANU/SC/2978/2006 : (2006)IIILLJ783SC . See also Kendriya Vidyalaya Sangathan and Ors. v. Sajal Kumar Roy and Ors. MANU/SC/8576/2006 : (2006)8SCC671 .

For the reasons aforementioned, the impugned judgment cannot be sustained. It is set aside accordingly. The Appeal is allowed. In the facts and circumstances of this case, however, there shall be no order as to costs.

NINETEEN

STATE BANK OF INDIA AND ORS. VS. SOMVIR SINGH, 2007

Hon'ble Judges/Coram:

H.K. Sema and B. Sudershan Reddy, JJ.

Equivalent Citation: 2007(3)ALD60(SC), 2007(3)ALLMR(SC)338, 2007(5)ALT1(SC), 2007 (2) AWC 1552 (SC), [2007(113)FLR225], JT2007(3)SC398, (2007)IILLJ230SC, 2007(2)PLJR46, 2007(3)SCALE42, (2007)4SCC778, (2007)2SCC(LS)92, [2007]2SCR509, 2007(2)SCT243(SC), 2007(3)SLR497(SC), 2007(2)WLN43, MANU/SC/7095/2007

Relevant Section: Article 16 of Constitution of India

Number of Pages in the Original Judgment: 05

Ratio Decidendi:

"Appointment - Compassionate grounds -Judicial review- Only question need to be decided by High Court is whether decision making process rejecting claim of respondent for compassionate appointment vitiated and Whether order not in conformity with scheme framed by appellant Bank "

Case Note:

i. Employment - Compassionate appointment--Whether when scheme of appellant Bank on compassionate appointment provided for consideration of financial position of family of deceased employee to arrive at conclusion whether family was in penury and without any means of livelihood and when conclusion was in negative, Bank justified in refusing compassionate appointment?--Held, "yes"--Such appointment cannot be claimed de hors scheme or statutory provisions--Whether High Court justified in interfering on ground that income of family not sufficient to take it out from penury?--Held, "no"--High Court could not have taken exercise to decide as to what would be reasonable income sufficient for family for its survival--Impugned order set aside.

ii. Constitution of India--Article 16 -- Employment -- Article 16 guarantees to all citizens equality of opportunity -- Dependants of employees dying-in-harness--Do not have any special or additional claim to public services other than one conferred, if any, by employer.

iii. Article 16 (1) of the Constitution of India guarantees to all its citizens equality of opportunity in matters relating to employment or appointment to any office under the State. Article 16 (2) protects citizens against discrimination in respect of any employment or office under the State on grounds only of religion, race, caste, sex, descent. It is so well-settled and needs no restatement at our ends that appointment on compassionate grounds is an exception carved out to the general rule that recruitment to public services is to be made in a transparent and accountable manner providing opportunity to all eligible persons to compete and participate in the selection process. Such appointments are required to be made on the basis of open invitation of applications and merit. Dependants of employees dying in harness do not have any special or additional claim to public services other than the one conferred, if any, by the employer.

Brief Facts:

i. The sole respondent is the son of Zile Singh who died while in harness on May 5, 1998. He was serving as an Assistant (typist/clerk) in the appellants-State Bank of India (hereinafter referred to as appellant-Bank). The respondent's mother submitted an application requesting the appellant-Bank for appointment of respondent by way of compassionate appointment. The respondent at the relevant time was studying in his matriculation examination. The Zonal Office of the appellant-Bank at Chandigarh required the family of the deceased employee to furnish the details of assets/pension/loan/income and other details as are required in order to consider the compassionate appointment. The same were furnished by the respondent. The Deputy General Manager of the Bank submitted the proposal for the consideration of the Competent Authority in the printed format inter alia indicating the details regarding the deceased employee, terminal benefits, details of immovable property left behind him, investments and liabilities as well as pension paid. The Deputy General Manager while forwarding the request for consideration of the Chief General Manager observed that the family of late Zile Singh has reasonable source of income to sustain itself and therefore, the request for appointment on compassionate ground does not qualify for favourable consideration. No doubt, the Branch Manager where the deceased employee was working recommended the case for appointment on compassionate ground. The Chief General Manager having regard to the financial condition of the family found that the resources of the family are adequate to meet its basic needs and accordingly rejected the request for appointment on compassionate grounds. The Competent Authority found that the financial condition of the family does not justify any such appointment on compassionate grounds. The order of the Chief General Manager in detail reveals that the deceased employee was entitled to Rs. 03.15 lacs towards terminal benefits and investments out of which Rs. 02.52 lacs were deducted towards the liabilities leaving net surplus of Rs. 00.63 lacs. The monthly family income included family pension drawn from the Bank at Rs. 2,214/- and income on agricultural land being Rs. 584/-. The family members are living in their own house. The value of the agricultural land possessed by the family has been fixed at Rs. 7 lacs. It is under those circumstances the Bank found that the family of the deceased employee had not been left in penury or without any means of livelihood.

ii. Challenging the order of rejection, the respondent filed a writ petition in Punjab and Haryana High Court. The Division Bench held that the income of Rs. 2,798/- "could not be treated to be an amount for the family which could be termed as such amount to take out the family from penury." The High Court accordingly directed the appellant-Bank to reconsider the claim of the petitioner for compassionate appointment keeping in view the entire facts and circumstances of the case and the observations made in the order. The order of the High Court is challenged in this appeal.

Held, while allowing the appeal:

i. In our considered opinion the High Court itself could not have undertaken any exercise to decide as to what would be the reasonable income which would be sufficient for the family for its survival and whether it had been left in penury or without any means of livelihood. The only question the High Court could have adverted itself is whether the decision making process rejecting the claim of the respondent for compassionate appointment is vitiated? Whether the order is not in conformity with the scheme framed by the appellant-Bank? It is not even urged that the order passed by the Competent Authority is not in accordance with the scheme. It is well settled that the hardship of the dependant does not entitle one to compassionate appointment de hors the scheme or the statutory provisions as the case may be. The income of the family from all sources is required to be taken into consideration according to scheme which the High Court altogether ignored while remitting the matter for fresh consideration by the appellant-Bank. It is not a case where the dependants of the deceased employee are left 'without any means of livelihood' and unable to make both ends meet. The High Court ought not to have disturbed the finding and the conclusion arrived at by the appellant- Bank that the respondent was not living hand to mouth. As observed by this Court in **General Manager (D&PB) and Ors.** v. **Kunti Tiwary and Anr.** MANU/SC/0891/2004 : (2004)IIILLJ1136SC , the High Court cannot dilute the criteria 'of penury to one of' "not very well-to-do". The view taken by the Division Bench of the High Court may amount to varying the existing scheme framed by the appellant-Bank. Such a course is impermissible in law.
ii. For all the aforesaid reasons, we allow the appeal filed by the appellant-Bank and set aside the order passed by the Division Bench of the High Court of Punjab and Haryana. There shall be no order as to costs.

TWENTY

ABHISHEK KUMAR VS. STATE OF HARYANA AND ORS., 2006

Hon'ble Judges/Coram:

S.B. Sinha and Markandey Katju, JJ.

Equivalent Citation: 2007(51)AIC68, 2007(3)ALT28(SC), 2006(5)ESC175(SC), [2007(112)FLR700], 2006(13)SCALE658, (2006)12SCC44, (2007)2SCC(LS)308, [2006]Supp(10)SCR37, 2007(2)SCT457(SC), 2007(3)SLR836(SC), MANU/SC/8801/2006

Relevant Section: Rule 9 of Haryana Compassionate Assistance to the Dependents of Deceased Government Employees Rules, 2003

Number of Pages in the Original Judgment: 02

Case Note:

Service - Appointment - Compassionate ground - Rule 9 of Haryana Compassionate Assistance to the Dependents of Deceased Government Employees Rules, 2003 -- Appellant had sought for appointment on compassionate grounds when 2003 Rules were not in existence - Held, case was required to be considered in terms of Rules existed in year 2001 - Appellant entitled to obtain appointment on compassionate grounds - When a Statewide list is prepared, it does not tie in mouth of authority incharge, be it District Magistrate or any other officer, to disobey order passed by higher Authority - Appellant willing to Join anywhere within State - State directed to issue appointment letter posting appellant to any post within State as per his original seniority - Appeal allowed.

Brief Facts:

The appellant's father expired on 10.2.2001 while in office. In terms of the Rule, as it was existing then, the appellant was entitled to be appointed on compassionate grounds. An application for such an appointment was filed within two weeks by the appellant from the date of his father's death. Not only the appellant was denied appointment in District Yamuna Nagar although his deceased father had been employed as a Kammgo in District Yamuna Nagar when he was sought to be appointed in the District of Karnal, the same was denied to him by the District Magistrate, Kamal Inter alia on the plea that there does not exist any vacancy.

Held, while allowing the appeal:

i. Appellant herein had sought for appointment on compassionate grounds at a point of time when 2003 Rules were not in existence. His case, therefore, was required to be considered in terms of the Rules which were in existence in the year 2001. Evidently, in the State of Haryana a State wise list is maintained. In terms of the said list so maintained by the State of Haryana, the appellant was entitled to obtain an appointment on compassionate grounds. He was offered such an appointment by the State. It was the District Magistrate who came on the way and refused to provide for the post. The High Court unfortunately failed to consider this aspect of the matter.
ii. When a Statewide list is prepared, it does not tie in the mouth of a authority incharge, be it a District Magistrate or any other officer, to disobey the order passed by a higher Authority. Furthermore, there might not be any post available at Karnal but there cannot be any doubt or dispute that such a post would be available in some other district within the State of Haryana as otherwise such an appointment could not have been made. The appellant in his written statement has categorically stated that he is ready and willing to Join anywhere in the State of Haryana.
iii. Before us the State has not filed any counter affidavit. The District Magistrate of Karnal has done so and before us also only the pleas which were raised before the High Court have been raised.
iv. For the reasons aforementioned, we are not inclined to accept the said pleas of respondent No. 4. We, therefore, allow this appeal and set aside the judgment of the High Court. The Department of Personnel, State of Haryana is directed to issue an appointment letter posting the appellant to any post within the State of Haryana as per his original seniority

within four weeks from the date of receipt of copy of this order.

Videos & Tv Shows On Law & Exim

List of some important videos & TV shows on Law & EXIM by Adv. Jayprakash Somani on his YouTube Channel 'Jayprakash Somani EXIM & Legal'

Legal Videos: Hindi -English

1) SLP in Supreme Court / Special Leave Petitions in the Supreme Court of India

2) Transfer of Civil & Criminal Cases by the Supreme Court of India / Transfer of Matrimonial Cases

3) Appellate Jurisdiction of the Supreme Court of India

4) Jurisdictions of the Supreme Court of India

5) Public Interest Litigation in the Supreme Court of India / PIL in Supreme Court

6) Article 32 Writ Petitions in the Supreme Court of India

7) Bail Matters Top 10 Supreme Court Cases

8) FIR Quashing in High Court & Supreme Court

9) Bail & Anticipatory Bail Matters in Supreme Court

10) Insolvency & Bankruptcy Matters in the Supreme Court

11) Insolvency & Bankruptcy Code 2016 Part 1

12) Insolvency & Bankruptcy Code 2016 Part 2

13) Insolvency & Bankruptcy Code 2016 Part 3

14) Corporate Liquidation Process

15) Supreme Court Rules & Procedures Webinar of 2.5 hour on Zoom

16) RDDBFI Act, 1993 (Introduction)

17) The Indian Contact Act 1872

18) Negotiable Instruments Act (Introduction)

19) How to avoid matrimonial disputes& some more videos

20)SEBI Matters in the Supreme Court

21) Matrimonial Matters: Supreme Court's 20 Case Laws

22) Consumer Matters Supreme Court's 20 Case Laws

23) Service Matters Supreme Court's 20 Case Laws

24) How to Search Lawyer for Your Matter

25) Property Matters Supreme Court's 20 Case Laws

26) Bail Matters: Supreme Court's 20 Case Laws

27) Supreme Court / High Court Vacation Benches

28)69000 Teacher's Recruitment Matters of UP Government in the Supreme Court

29) Contempt of Court Matters in the Supreme Court

30) Advocate Act's Matters in the Supreme Court

31) Business Law Matters in the Supreme Court

32) Banking Matters in the Supreme Court

33) Labour Law Matters in the Supreme Court

34) Arbitration Matters in the Supreme Court

35) Careers in Law -Zoom Webinar by Adv. Jayprakash Somani

36) Civil Matters in the Supreme Court

37) Consumer Protection Act | Consumer Matters in the Supreme Court

38) Corporate Matters in the Supreme Court

39) Criminal Matters in the Supreme Court

40) Role of Respondent in the Supreme Court of India

41) Motor Vehicle Accident Matters in Supreme Court with case laws

42) Article 131 Original Suits in Supreme Court

43)PIL in Supreme Court/ Public Interest Litigations in the Supreme Court of India'

44)CAB Citizenship Amendment Bill is not Unconstitutional

45) Supreme Court of India Cases & Process – Marathi

46) Legal Services Export / Export of Legal Services

47) Transfer of Matrimonial Cases by the Supreme Court of India

48) Public Interest Litigation PIL

49) The Specific Relief Act (Introduction)

50) Corporate Insolvency Resolution Process CIRP

51)ABMM's Career 5 - Careers in Law

52) Transfer of cases by Supreme Court

53) Writ Petitions in High Court & Supreme Court of India

54) Supreme Court Jurisdictions - Appeals, SLP, Writ Petitions, Transfer, Original, Review, Curative

55)LEGAL INDIA TV Show: Cases Handled in Supreme Court

56) Corporate Liquidation Process

57) Legal Services Export / Export of Legal Services

PPP

EXIM Videos: Hindi -English

1) Yes, I can do Import Export Business Easily! 36 points excellent video in Hindi

2) Yes, I can do Import Export Business Easily! 36 points excellent video in English

3) Import Export Business – Hindi video

4) Import Export Business - English video

5) Export Import Marathi TV Interview

6) Scope for Commerce Students in International Business- TV Show

7) Scope for Management Student in International Business- TV Show

8) Scope for Engineering Students in International Business – TV Show

9) Women in International Business- TV Show

10) How to do Import Export Business Successfully!‘

11) Where one can get full information on Import Export Business?

12) What to do import & export?

13) Import Export Workshop/ Training/Course/ Diploma

14) How to Start Import Export Business & How to grow it. Live Webinar

15) Success Stories & Failure Stories in Import & Export Business

16) For MSME Scope in Export & Import...

17) Exports In Agri. & Food Products – English & some more videos

18) Exports to Dubai, Aabudhabii. e. UAE

19) Jewelry Exports from India

20) How to attend EXIM workshop to become excellent Exporter

21) Import Export Best Training Course – Online & Offline

22) Agri Product Export

23) Scope for Woman in International Business

24) Management Graduates Scope in International Business

25) Pharma Product's Export

26) Best Import Export Course | Practical Training | Aaronica Global Exim

27) Import Export Business for Commerce Graduates

28) How Do I Get Export Orders? Finding International Buyers

29) What Is APEDA In Import Export Business?

30) Which Is The Best Product To Export From India?

31)EXIM Remark by Manoj Kumar Faridabad

32)EXIM Remarks by Mahesh Telangana

33) What Licenses I Need To Start Import/ Export?

34) How Can I Increase My Import Export Business?

35) Which Is Best B2B Website For Import/Export Business?

36) Export Import Management with Global Marketing

37) How to Start Export Import Business | 51 Points Video

38) Scope for Commerce & Other Graduates in International Business

39)BE A SUCCESSFUL EXPORTER FOR OUR NATION - Marathi video

40) Export of Textile , Cotton, Agri., Food, & other products & services

41) Exports from MP, CG, MH, GJ & CA in Fresh Fruits & Vegetables

42) Exports in Agri. & Food Products- Hindi

43) Start your Online/E-Commerce Business

44) How to Start Export Import Business & Grow it

45) Exports in Textile & Other Products

46) Start and grow EXIM business - Live English Webinar

47)'Import Export Business!' Why, Who, What &How can one do it easily!!

48) Live: Export of Product & Services During & After Lock Down Period

49) Frauds in Import Export Business

50) Import Export for Business Man

51) Import& Export for Women

51) Import& Export for Graduate & Post - Graduate Students

52) Agriculture Exports from India

53) Digital Marketing Setup - Marathi

54)2nd Secret of Successful Businessman

55) Digital Marketing Set up

56) Legal Services Export / Export of Legal Services

57) Export& Import with UAE

58) Service Exports / Exports by Service Providers

59) Import Export Workshop/ Training/Course/ Diploma

60) Exports& Imports with USA

61) Selection on Product for Export

62) Top Products Exported from India

63) What to do import & export?

64)ABMM Career 2 - 'Careers in Business & Industries

65) How to do Import Export Business Successfully!'

66)5 Secrets of Successful Businessman

67) Export from MP, Chhattisgarh &Vidarbha Nagpur

68)EXIM Hindi - Textile & Apparel Export

69)EXIM Hindi - Export Import Practical Training In Delhi, Kolkata, Mumbai and Pune

70) Import Export Business

71) Import Export Business Hindi

72) Import Export Business English video

73) Import Export Business Marathi

74) Women in International Business by Exim Guru Adv. Jayprakash Somani

75) Opportunities in Foreign Trade- Adv. Jayprakash Somani's special interview

List Of Adv. Jayprakash Somani's Books

1. Supreme Court of India's Leading Case Laws on 'Insolvency & Bankruptcy Code 2016'

2. Bail Matters – Supreme Court's Latest Leading Case Laws

3. Arbitration Matters- Supreme Court's Latest Leading Case Laws

4. Property Matters - Supreme Court's Latest Leading Case Laws

5. Matrimonial Matters- Supreme Court's Latest Leading Case Laws

6. Election Matters- Supreme Court's Latest Leading Case Laws

7.SEBI Matters- Supreme Court's Latest Leading Case Laws

8. Banking Matters- Supreme Court's Latest Leading Case Laws

9. Service Matters- Supreme Court's Latest Leading Case Laws

10. Contempt of Court Matters- Supreme Court's Latest Leading Case Laws

11. Consumer Protection Matters- Supreme Court's Latest Leading Case Laws

12. Corporate Law- Supreme Court's Latest Leading Case Laws

13. Supreme Court's AOR Exam- Leading Cases

14. Armed Force Tribunal - Supreme Court's Latest Leading Case Laws

15. Acquittal From 376 - Supreme Court's Latest Leading Case Laws

16. Negotiable instrument – Supreme Court's Latest Leading Case Laws

17. Contract Act- Supreme Court's Latest Leading Case Laws

18. Insider trading- Supreme Court's Latest Leading Case Laws

19. Foreign Exchange and Management Act- Supreme Court's Latest Leading Case Laws

20. Income Tax Act- Supreme Court's Latest Leading Case Laws

21. Company Law- Supreme Court's Latest Leading Case Laws

22. Competition & Monopoly Matters- Supreme Court's Latest Leading Case Laws

23. Compulsory Retirement- Service Matters- Supreme Court's Latest Leading Case Laws

24. Compassionate Appointment- Service Matters- Supreme Court's Latest Leading Case Laws

These Books are available online at

1. **Notion Press:** https://notionpress.com/author/jayprakash_somani
2. **Amazon:** https://www.amazon.in/s?k=jayprakash+somani
3. **Flipkart:** https://www.flipkart.com/search?q=Jayprakash%20Somani

9 798885 691895

Printed by Libri Plureos GmbH in Hamburg,
Germany